IMAGES
of England

BILSTON, TETTENHALL AND WEDNESFIELD

IMAGES
of England

BILSTON, TETTENHALL AND WEDNESFIELD

Compiled by
Mary Mills and Tracey Williams

TEMPUS

First published 1998
Copyright © Wolverhampton Borough Council, 1998

Tempus Publishing Limited
The Mill, Brimscombe Port,
Stroud, Gloucestershire, GL5 2QG

ISBN 0 7524 1569 7

Typesetting and origination by
Tempus Publishing Limited
Printed in Great Britain by
Midway Clark Printing, Wiltshire

Front cover photograph: Sankey's staff, around 1940 (see page 35).

Contents

Acknowledgments

All of the photographs used in this book come from the collection at Wolverhampton Archives and Local Studies, 42-50 Snow Hill, Wolverhampton WV2 4AG. The collection has been built up from a variety of sources and, where these are known, acknowledgements are given below each photograph. Every effort has been made to ensure accuracy and we apologise if anyone has inadvertently been missed. The reference numbers given at the end of the captions are those of Wolverhampton Archives and Local Studies.

The authors would like to thank their colleagues, Caroline Sampson, Jonathan Everall, Joanna Shepherd and Veronica Morrall, for their help and support during the compilation of this book. Thanks also to Janice Endean and the staff at Eardley Lewis Photography.

Introduction

1966 and all that!

On 1 April 1966 the new County Borough of Wolverhampton came into existence under the West Midlands Order 1965. This new borough consisted of the whole of the previous County Borough, together with the borough of Bilston, the urban districts of Tettenhall and Wednesfield, parts of the urban districts of Coseley, Sedgley, Darlaston and Willenhall and parts of the parishes of Lower Penn, Wombourne, Wrottesley, Brewood and Essington.

The process of change had started nine years earlier in November 1957 with the publication of the Local Government Bill revealing six 'review areas' - five in the provinces and one in Greater London. The Local Government Commission was to oversee investigations and proposed that five new county boroughs ('the big five') should be created in the Black Country - Dudley, Smethwick, Walsall, West Bromwich and Wolverhampton. Each of the five would take in part of the surrounding area which, in the case of Wolverhampton, included the existing borough of Bilston and the urban districts of Tettenhall and Wednesfield. All of these were two-tier authorities at the time, carrying out some functions themselves but also looking to Staffordshire County Council for some local authority services.

Feelings ran high across the whole of the Black Country, particularly in the smaller areas which feared being swallowed up by 'greedy neighbours', losing their civic pride and separate identity in the process. Staffordshire County Council accepted that there were too many small authorities in the Black Country but it objected to the Commission's proposals and came up with an alternative plan for some of the smaller boroughs and urban districts to amalgamate with each other, for example Bilston would have merged with Tipton whilst Wednesfield would have amalgamated with Willenhall. Wednesbury and Darlaston councils suggested another alternative - a central county borough with an administrative centre in Moxley and consisting of themselves, together with Bilston, Tipton, Willenhall and Coseley.

Bilston was at the time a town of 33,500 people and was a borough in its own right. A campaign was launched under the slogan 'Bilston for the Bilstonians' and in June 1961 a group of businessmen formed the Bilston Defence Committee. Within sixteen hours of its formation the committee delivered a coffin to Bilston Town Hall to symbolize the threatened death of the town. A deposit was made on a plot of land in Hickman Park so that this coffin, containing Bilston's 'soul' in the form of historical documents relating to the town's former life, could be buried if the proposed merger with Wolverhampton took place.

Tettenhall's argument for staying out of Wolverhampton was that 'naturally and historically' it formed no part of the Black Country and should not be involved in any changes to local government in the area. It was felt that there was 'no community of interest ... between it and Wolverhampton beyond physical proximity and the social and economic ties which exist between any large centre and its surrounding area'. The view was expressed that it was not a suburb of Wolverhampton and had grown up as a village community with a history as long as that of Wolverhampton. It was felt that Tettenhall would be able to merge more successfully with the Seisdon Rural District.

Wednesfield UDC said that it believed in two-tier government and wanted to stay as it was. It also rejected the County Council's scheme which would have seen it merge with Willenhall. Like Tettenhall, it had managed to survive previous attempts by Wolverhampton to extend the borough boundaries. Housing was said by Wednesfield to be the 'Trojan Horse' that had been introduced into the urban district over the past few years in the shape of overspill from Wolverhampton. Running out of land on which to build new houses, Wolverhampton had agreements with Tettenhall for four sites, dating from 1947, and also with Wednesfield. It seemed to the two urban districts that Wolverhampton was then using the reclamation of its overspill population as one excuse to extend its boundaries.

Wolverhampton's view was that the Local Government Commission's proposals would result in a simple, strong and coherent system of government, replacing a patchwork of more than twenty local authorities with five, each of them capable of discharging a whole range of local government activities. A note of caution was sounded in 1962 by the Vicar of Bushbury, Revd C.A. Chamberlain, who had lived in Wolverhampton for six years and feared that the closely-knit town which had so impressed him could lose its spirit and become a soulless community if it swallowed up its neighbouring populations.

The Commission set great store by continuous development and said that Bilston, Wednesfield and Tettenhall were all linked to Wolverhampton by continuous urban development. Much of the population of these areas worked in Wolverhampton and this was also taken into account by the Commissioners. The Minister for Housing and Local Government, Sir Keith Joseph, recognised that Tettenhall, Sedgley and Brierley Hill were to some extent different in character from the typical industrial districts at the heart of the Black Country but said 'it is right that they should be included in its local government system as they are essentially bound up with the area and dependent on its prosperity. It cannot be satisfactory that the more prosperous residential areas of a town should be administratively separate from its working centre when the whole is of a size to form a convenient unit of local government'.

Following the announcement in August 1962 that the 'Big Five' county boroughs would be created, the unhappy boroughs and urban districts vowed to carry on fighting. The proposals were set to take effect from 1 April 1964 but the decision of Wednesbury, Darlaston, Bilston, Willenhall and Sedgley councils to contest the legality of the Local Government Commission inquiry considerably delayed events. The councils' High Court action took place in May 1965 and when the ruling was made that the inquiry was valid, the councils decided to go to the Court of Appeal. In July 1965 the five towns lost the appeal battle and were refused leave to appeal to the House of Lords. Still undaunted, the five towns persevered until October 1965 but were then forced to accept that the fight was finally over. The West Midlands Order 1965 was approved by Parliament on 16 December 1965 to come into effect on 1 April 1966.

The feeling of Bilston, Tettenhall and Wednesfield councils was that they had done what they could and now just had to resign themselves to the situation. The retiring Mayor of Bilston, Councillor Harold Humphries, summed up the feelings of many in December 1965, 'We have made our protest - unsuccessfully - so now we are going to do our damnedest to make this merger work. We have had a very fair deal from Wolverhampton on this matter. Now we are only anxious that we should be well-represented on the new council'. The Mayor of Wolverhampton expressed his appreciation of this positive attitude and agreed, 'It is to the future we must look ... all that is needed now is a determination by all concerned to make the enlarged county borough function successfully'.

Whatever the feelings about the administrative changes which happened in 1966, there can be no doubt that, more than thirty years later, the one thing that all of the areas dreaded has not happened. The populations of Bilston, Tettenhall and Wednesfield all feared that the character of their areas would be destroyed if they became part of Wolverhampton. The fact that each area still retains its own distinct identity and pride is a testament to the spirit of those who have met the challenge with goodwill and co-operation whilst retaining the individual approach and tradition of their community.

One
Bilston

The Charter Day service in Hickman Park on 28 September 1933.

Bilston today has grown out of the three communities of Bilston, Bradley and Ettingshall, all of which are referred to in the Domesday Book. Situated on the old road from London to Holyhead, Bilston was one of the largest villages in England when it became a market town by an Act of Parliament in 1824.

The town stands on slightly elevated ground, 2 ½ miles south-east of Wolverhampton. Described in 1700 as a large and beautiful village containing a great number of beautiful half-timbered houses, the Bilston we know today is very much a product of the Industrial Revolution. Its location on the 30ft seam of 'thick coal' above and below which were valuable strata of ironstone, gave it the natural resources to exploit developments in industry.

The proximity of the coal to the surface in the Bilston area enabled the open-cast system of mining to be practised until late in the nineteenth century. These rich deposits of iron and coal, which could be easily and cheaply worked, together with limestone from the neighbouring hills, secured Bilston's fortune as a centre of the iron and coal trade in the Black Country.

Many of the great names and discoveries of the Industrial Revolution were associated with the Bilston district. The first equipment for de-watering mines was installed on the coalfield by Savery in the early seventeenth century and Newcomen's first atmospheric steam engine was erected in 1712 at a coal pit in the Bilston/Dudley area (exact location unknown). However, it was the arrival of John Wilkinson in Bradley in 1756 which led to Bilston becoming the most important town on the South Staffordshire Coalfield. Wilkinson established his first blast furnace for the manufacture of pig iron in 1767, doubling his output with the installation of a Boulton and Watt steam engine in 1775. In 1784 he also applied and then adapted Henry Cort's invention of the puddling furnace and rolling mill.

During the eighteenth and nineteenth centuries, pig and wrought iron were both produced at Bilston in ever-increasing quantities. As mining and iron smelting activities grew, so did other manufacturing industries related to them and Bilston became an important centre for the subsidiary trades of japanning, sheet metal, galvanizing, tin plate and the manufacture of a wide range of domestic hardware.

New factories and mines sprang up alongside the Birmingham Canal, begun in 1767 by James Brindley. The canal forms an exaggerated loop south of Bilston, probably in order to take in the area covered by the coal and iron works at Bradley. By 1841 the population of Bilston had reached 20,181, a huge increase on the population of 6,914 only forty years earlier. This is despite the cholera which ravaged the town in 1832, resulting in the deaths of over 700 people – 5% of the total population. Whole streets were depopulated and coffins had to be brought by cart from Birmingham as they could not be made quickly enough in Bilston. After about 1860, the population began to decrease and the town's prosperity began to decline.

Coal and iron were so easily extracted that the coalfield was exploited to the full and by 1860 signs of exhaustion were apparent. Approximately 10% of Bilston's population were colliers and every available plot of land for iron or coal was extensively exploited. As well as open-cast mining, the bell system of sinking shafts, which were then widened or belled out at the bottom, was extensively used. As the bell became wider and subsidence became a greater possibility, the shaft was abandoned and a new one begun nearby. By this means, the natural drainage of the underground workings was rapidly destroyed and, in 1873, the South Staffordshire Mines Drainage Act was passed, allowing a Commission to investigate problems of flooding and arrange for the pumping of an area.

The decline of the iron trade in Bilston was due not only to the exhaustion of supply but also to the establishment of new centres of production such as Middlesborough and, in the later part of the nineteenth century, to foreign competition. The invention of basic steel by Bessemer and improvements in steel processes meant that steel replaced iron in a number of uses. Bilston steelworks specialised in high quality carbon and low alloy steels, mainly for the production of seamless tubes. During the Second World War Bilston became an important centre for shell production and supplied steel for Pluto - Pipeline Under The Ocean - which carried fuel supplies to Allied troops. By the 1960s Bilston had the only integrated iron and steel plant in the West Midlands.

The heavy manufacturing and metal bashing industries which brought prosperity to Bilston up to the post-war boom of the 1950s and 60s left the town vulnerable to the economic downturn which followed in the recession of the 1970s and 80s. The key to recovery is the diversification of the area's economic base, encouraging a mix of investment so that the balance between the manufacturing and service sectors moves more towards the national norm.

Bilston Coat of Arms. The coat of arms was granted in 1933 when the town was incorporated as a borough. The arms were based upon those of Sir Walter de Bilston (thirteenth century) which were formerly used by Bilston Urban District Council. The arms are: Ermine, a black bend and thereon a gold fess between two silver martlets, and on the fess a red Stafford knot. The crest is described as: on a white and black wreath, the rising sun, gold, in front of three green oak leaves. The supporters are Faith, represented by a woman in a blue robe and bearing a lamp; and Industry in the guise of Vulcan wearing a red tunic and bearing a hammer. The motto is 'Fidelitate et Industria stat Bilstonia' - 'Bilston stands by Faith and Industry'

No. 62 Ash Street, c.1910. The home of Mr and Mrs R. Smallshire, pictured here with two relatives. Mr Smallshire was a cabinet maker and used the building on the left as a workshop. The house was demolished in 1967. (Mr J. Smallshire)

A busy, prosperous High Street, around the 1930s. Note the trolleybus wires overhead. Until the nineteenth century High Street and Church Street formed the main through road of the town, carrying traffic from Wolverhampton to Wednesbury. (C1/HIG/7/7)

High Street in 1968 showing the Elisabeth blast furnace of Bilston Steelworks. Replacing three smaller blast furnaces, 'Big Lizzie' was first lit in 1954. By tradition, after relining, the furnace had to be relit by a young girl. The only time it was lit by a man, the furnace went out. By the time the 1,600 ton Elisabeth was brought down in October 1980, she was the last blast furnace in the area. (C1/HIG/7/3)

Ash Street in 1928 with Daisy Bank school on the right. During the excavation of trenches for laying sewers in the street, coal was exposed and the picture shows local people sorting through the coal which was very close to the surface. (Mr J. Smallshire)

Swan Bank, *c.* 1910. On the right is the Town Hall, built on the corner of Church Street and Swan Bank in the 1870s. Other noticeable buildings are Lloyd's ironmongers, E. & A. Ashley's confectioners, Frisby's boot stores and T.H. Plant & Sons, Spirit Vaults. (C1/SWAN/5/1)

Barclays Bank, Swan Bank in the early twentieth century with tramlines for the Lorain trams visible in the foreground. (L7/BARC/E/1)

Church Street in the early 1950s, photographed from the roof of the Market Hall, with Marks & Spencers on the left. (Mr A. Wootton)

A view of Church Street in the early 1900s. Wood Street is on the left and the building on the corner is the former residence of the Perry family.

Oxford Street, near Hare Street. At No. 138 was Herbert Holloway, greengrocer and the shop with the two women outside was Pritchard's sweet shop. The street was cut in the 1820s and became the turnpike road to Wednesbury. By the late nineteenth century it had become a thriving area with shops, pubs and four churches - Anglican, Methodist, Congregational and Roman Catholic.

Oxford Street in 1960 with Railway Street on the right. An article in the *Express & Star* on 17 June 1968 laments the decline of Oxford Street, citing problems of waste ground and empty and derelict shops. Local shopkeepers commented that the slow decline began in the late 1950s as a result of the street no longer being the focal point of the town. Wolverhampton Council in the same article outlined plans for improved housing development in the area and said that, although shops and offices at the top end of the road were safe, there were no plans for the street to be a shopping centre. (*Wolverhampton Chronicle*)

A postcard view of Mount Pleasant, Bilston from around the 1950s. The street was once home to some of Bilston's wealthier residents such as the Bruetons but it also became a thriving commercial area with shops, such as Hartills, clearly visible here. (C1/MOU/8/2)

A Lorain tram travels down Wellington Road in this postcard view from the early part of this century. According to a Bilston guide book of 1948, the first trees in Wellington Road were planted in 1876 in an effort to beautify the area. It is interesting to note that some of the residents of this road also owned a number of properties in the slum clearance areas. (Mr Rhodes, C2/WELL/0/7)

18

Best Road, Green Lanes in around 1949. (C2/BES/0/1)

A John Price & Sons postcard of Etheridge Road at its junction with Marchant Road. Etheridge Road, like Etheridge School, was named after John Etheridge (1772-1856) a local businessman and philanthropist who lived in Church Street. (John Price & Sons (Printers) Ltd, C2/ETH/0/2)

Villiers Avenue from another postcard by the Bilston firm of John Price & Sons. The tennis club, established in 1895, is on the left. The street was described in a guide book of 1948 as a pleasant residential thoroughfare. (John Price & Sons (Printers) Ltd, C2/VILL/0/1)

Frazer Street in 1918. Etheridge School is to the left.

A rare view of the interior of a house in 1963. No. 66 Willenhall Road was the home of Mrs Clara Jones and the photograph shows a range which was made by Lathe of Tipton. (Roy D. Salter)

Queen Street, showing typical advertisements for everyday products.

Coseley Road and Prosser Street. These buildings were subject to No. 3 Clearance Order 1934 and were subsequently demolished. In the 1930s Bilston carried out inspections on a large number of properties to determine whether they were fit for habitation, being mostly free from damp, satisfactorily lighted and ventilated, in good repair with a satisfactory water supply, washing accommodation and sanitary arrangements. Any buildings which were deemed to be unfit and which could not reasonably be repaired became the subject of clearance orders and were demolished.

Chapel Street and Bradley Street Clearance Order 1934 showed thirty seven occupiers in the eight houses scheduled for demolition. The 'court' system of building houses round a central courtyard at the back of main streets was typical of densely populated areas such as Bilston and Wolverhampton where demand for housing was such that all available space was used.

Hare Street, off Oxford Street, probably in the 1930s. (C1/HARE/0/1)

Greencroft contained another group of houses deemed unfit for habitation. An inspector's report on eleven of the houses in the street in October 1934 described the sanitary conditions. There were only four water closets to serve the six houses fronting the street and the five in the yard at the rear. The water supply consisted of one stand pipe in the yard with one tap in each of two wash-houses. Tenants of these houses were paying rent of between 4/7 and 6/5 per week. Owners of properties, in some cases reported as being in circumstances little better than their tenants, were permitted to increase the rent by 25% to allow for repairs. However, it seems that a large number of houses in the Bilston district had net rents of 3/- and 4/- per week and the permitted increase was considered insufficient to carry out repairs. (C1/GREE/0/6)

Wolverhampton Street and Shale Street Clearance Order affected Nos. 57-75 Wolverhampton Street and 12-20 Shale Street, a total of sixteen houses and forty seven occupiers. (C1/WOL/0/4)

Coseley Road, 1934. A report of the Medical Officer of Health and Housing Inspector in October 1934 notes that three of the houses in the street had dangerous walls, roofs and chimneys and were liable to collapse. The council was advised to treat them as dangerous buildings and quickly demolish them rather than going through the usual procedures of issuing demolition notices which would take about three months. (Barnard Chatwin, C2/COSE/0/1)

Council houses being built in Hall Park Street in 1920. (C1/HALP/0/1)

More house-building taking place in Chettle Road and Martin Road, Bradley. (A2/BRAD/0/1)

No 1

Bilston Cemetery   Levelled Pit Bank Waste   Bilston Township

This, together with the following five photographs, is taken from a composite picture captioned, 'Panoramic view of Bilston - the view from Thompsons Boiler Yard'. This one gives a view towards the township of Bilston with Bilston cemetery on the left. The levelled pit bank waste shows the impact of mining activities on the area's landscape. (DX/6/103)

No 2

Millfields Iron Smelting Furnaces   Solmans Timber Yard

Claridges Foundry for Pipes &c   Millfields Forge & Rolling Mills   Bantocks Boat Dock

Levelled Pit Bank - Waste

Looking towards Millfields furnaces. A 1958 guidebook of Bilston says that the first blast furnace in the town was erected in 1767 by John Wilkinson and by 1790 it was reported that of twenty one blast furnaces in the whole of Britain, fifteen were in Bilston. In 1830 Bilston is said to have produced more iron in its blast furnaces, mills and foundries than Sweden which was at that time one of the foremost nations in Europe for iron-making. (DX/6/103)

No. 3

(c)
Church

Millfields House. Managers Residence   Galen Chemical Works   Barlows Mill and Piggeries

Sparrows Pig Iron Wharf   Woods Boat Yard

(c)

Looking towards Galen Chemical Works. (DX/6/103)

No. 4

Thompsons Boilers Manufactory   and Yard

Thompson's boiler manufactory and yard. The firm of John Thompson was founded around 1840 and was a pioneer in the production of Lancashire and other boilers. (DX/6/103)

No 5

Nail Rod & Wire Works

Woodalls Boiler Yard

Rolling Mills   Pit Bank Waste   Butlers Brewery   Priestfield

Looking towards Priestfields with Butlers Brewery in the centre. (DX/6/103)

No 6   View from Thompsons Boiler Yard looking down along Canal between Galon Co & Millfields Forge &c &c

Foundry   Rolling Mills   Smelting Furnaces   Boat Dock   Galen Wks

Looking down along the Birmingham Canal towards Millfields. (DX/6/103)

These cottages at Deepfields are is typical of the miners' cottages which were scattered around the area. A report from the Midland Mining Commission of 1843 describes the landscape, 'in some directions one may travel for miles and never be out of site of two storied houses ... interspersed with blazing furnaces, heaps of burning coal ... pit banks and engine chimneys ... These circumstances ... have effectually excluded from [the area] all classes except those whose daily bread depends upon their residence within the district'.

Coal mining in Moxley Road. A deed dated 1315 gives the first mention of coal pits in the area and mining operations gradually increased over the years. It was estimated that in 1864 no less than 10 million tons of coal were raised in the Bilston district. Much of the coal was extracted from the famous 'Thick Coal' or 'Ten Yard Seam' by shallow adits or pits.

An exterior view of the Springvale works which was purchased in 1866 by Alfred Hickman. It seems that iron had been made from blast furnaces on the site since the 1780s. The firms of Springvale Furnaces Ltd and the Staffordshire Steel and Ingot Iron Co., which were both on the same site, amalgamated in 1897 to form Alfred Hickman Ltd. In turn, this firm was taken over in 1920 by Stewarts & Lloyds and in 1962 the Wolverhampton & Birchley Rolling Mills was acquired. On nationalisation in 1967 Bilston steelworks became part of the British Steel Corporation, eventually becoming part of the Special Steels Division of the corporation. Steel-making on the site came to an end with the last cast on 12 April 1979 with the loss of 1,900 jobs. About 450 workers in the rolling mill and finishing plant remained at the works for a further year. (L6/BIL/E/2)

A dramatic photograph of a furnace being tapped, c.1976. A reporter visiting the steelworks in 1968 commented on the roaring, hissing and clattering ringing in his ears. Even after leaving the works he describes still feeling the blistering heat on his face and blinking from the blinding, searing light. The monstrous heat of up to 150 degrees in the summer meant that some men lived on salt tablets and a furnaceman, reportedly, could drink twenty pints of beer a day. (Nick Hedges, L6/BIL/I/67)

A blast furnace crew at Bilston steelworks, c.1976. All the steelmen were issued with flameproof clothing and wooden clogs. Shift working in teams meant that it was possible to work with basically the same people for ten years or more and some families had a steel tradition with several generations employed at the works. It was hard work but was supposed to be a job for life, one where you could work your way up. Except in wartime, women only worked in the offices, not on the shop floor. (Nick Hedges, L6/BIL/I/63)

A workshop at Bilston steelworks, probably in the 1950s. (L6/BIL/I/121)

Bilston steelworks training centre laboratory. The company built its own training centre and ran courses in conjunction with the education authority. (L6/BIL/I/125)

An early 1950s photograph of the Phoenix glass works of the British Heat-Resisting Glass Company in Loxdale Street, Bilston. On the left is Harry Barton blowing a glass tube, possibly for a strip light. (Mr A Wootton, L6/BRIH/I/1)

The installation of new electric ovens at the British Heat-Resisting Glass Co. on 8 May 1956. A town guidebook from 1958 describes the Phoenix brand glassware, designed by experts using new methods and mixtures, as 'easily washable, heat-resisting, virtually unmarkable and tasteful enough for the housewife to have on her table as well as in her kitchen'. (*Dudley Herald*)

The firm of Joseph Sankey & Sons Ltd began by making and japanning tea trays in the mid-1800s, expanding into the electrical lamination business in 1887. By the 1950s, Bankfield works was described as the largest and best-equipped in Europe for the production of laminations for the electrical and allied industries. Sankey's became part of the GKN group and, following the closure of Bilston steelworks, was Bilston's largest employer. However, hundreds of workers at the Albert Street brewery products, engineering works, vending machines and electrical laminations plant at Bankfields were made redundant during the 1980s in an effort to survive huge financial losses. The Morrisons superstore is now part of the GKN Sankey site. (L6/SAN/I/18)

A welcome break for tea at Sankey's, c.1940. (L6/SAN/I/1)

Women workers at Sankey's in the 1940s.
(L6/SAN/I/30)

Sankey's staff in the grounds of the staff canteen, c.1940. Second from right is Rene Hawthorn (nee Davies) and fifth from right is Mrs B. Richards.

Oxford Street in June 1913. In the doorway is Mrs T.E. Purshouse with her son and daughter. The newspaper headlines refer to the drama on Derby Day, 4 June 1913, when Emily Wilding-Davison, waving a suffragette flag, collided with the King's horse and died five days later. (P.J. Smith, C1/OXFO/0/5)

G.R. Underwood's shop in Bilston, before 1910. According to Kelly's Directory 1900 the shop was at 27 Oxford Street. There was also another shop in Tettenhall. (Margaret Singleton, L3/UNB/E/1)

Naylor's greengrocers at 158 Wellington Road, around the 1950s. (L3/NAY/E/1)

Thomas Swann's cycle shop at 69 High Street, taken soon after it opened in the early 1920s.
Tom Swann, demobbed from the Royal Flying Corps in 1918, can be seen in the doorway
wearing the 'britches' he used to wear to ride his 1914 Rudge motorbike. The shop was next
door to Fred King's fish and chip shop and sold bicycles, prams, pushchairs, wirelesses,
gramophones, electrical gear and toys. A second shop was later opened in Worcester Street,
Wolverhampton and the business was sold in the 1950s. (Mr B.T.B. Swann, L3/SWA/E/1)

Stonefield Girls' School in the early 1930s. Stonefield Secondary schools were founded in 1908 on the same site as the junior schools in Prosser Street. The boys and girls schools merged in 1965 and after 1970 merged with Broad Lanes Secondary to form Hall Green High School. This school was renamed The Bilston High School in 1992 and merged with Colton Hills School in 1994. (Mrs J.F. Bingle, I3/STO/I/2)

May Day celebrations at Stonefield Girls' School in 1932. (Mrs J.F. Bingle, I3/STO/I/6)

The Girls High School, Bilston. No 8

Bilston Girls' High School was founded in 1918/19 in Brueton House, Mount Pleasant (now the Library, Museum and Art Gallery) and moved to purpose built accommodation in Green Lanes in 1930. The building became a sixth form college in 1976 and since 1983/4 has housed Bilston Community College. (13/BGH/E/1)

A postcard view of the kindergarten class at Bilston Girls' High School. (John Price & Sons (Printers) Ltd, I3/BGH/I/2)

Pupils of Bilston Girls' High School in the gymnasium. (John Price & Sons (Printers) Ltd, I3/BGH/I/1)

PARISH CHURCH, BILSTON.

St Leonard's church, taken from Walsall Street in 1925. The church is known to have stood on its present site, the most elevated spot in the town, since the fourteenth century. Following some rebuilding and repair work in 1733 and 1744, the church was rebuilt in 1825-6. Designed by the London architect Francis Goodwin to a classical design, the cost of £9,235 was paid for by a rate levied on local inhabitants and a parliamentary grant of £550. During the rebuilding the congregation worshipped at Willenhall on Sunday mornings.

A Sunday school outing from Holy Trinity church, Ettingshall on 7 July 1956. (*Dudley Herald*)

A rear view of the Greyhound & Punchbowl, High Street, before its reconstruction in 1936. Built in approximately 1450 by John de Mollesley, the building is one of the oldest in Bilston and was originally called Stowheath Manor. The main front of the house faces south and would have been divided into three blocks: the west wing containing the principal living room, the east wing the kitchen area and a hall which connected the two. (A.E. Magna)

The Greyhound & Punchbowl following restoration in 1936. In 1820, the building became a public house and was very popular with local miners and foundry workers. Over the years the building fell into disrepair and by 1936 its condition was so bad that demolition became a real possibility. Fortunately, it was saved by W. Butler & Co. who purchased the building and carried out restoration work. (A.E. Magna)

The Leopard Inn, 97 Church Street in January 1934. The licensee at the time was Frank Pearman. The pub stood opposite the Cricketer's Arms, on a site which later became the TSB. The Leopard was demolished sometime around 1970. (W. Butler & Co.)

The interior of the Leopard Inn with Mr and Mrs J.R. Hughes in 1960. (W. Butler & Co., L4/LEO/I/1)

The Lord Nelson, on the corner of Bridge Street and Frazer Street, c.1950. This appears on a map of c.1900 simply as a beer house called the Nelson, one of three licensed houses in the street, the others being the Red Cow and the Three Tuns. The Lord Nelson was demolished around 1970. (Roy D. Salter)

The Tap Room at the Lord Nelson. (L4/NEL/I/1)

The White Lion in Temple Street in the 1930s. Within a radius of less than $\frac{3}{4}$ mile of St Leonard's church there were 113 houses licensed for the sale of intoxicating drinks at the turn of the century. This gave an average of one licensed house for every 140 inhabitants, a figure higher than that of cities such as Birmingham or Leeds. At the beginning of the nineteenth century about every fourth house in the main street was a pub. (W. Butler & Co.)

The Malt Shovel Inn, Oxford Street in November 1934. This stood between the Saddle & Stirrups and the Talbot. (W. Butler & Co.)

Mr and Mrs Nicholls at the Saddle & Stirrups, Oxford Street on the corner of Warwick Street. (L4/SAD/I/1)

The Brown Lion, 165 Oxford Street, pictured in 1953. The decorations suggest that the customers were celebrating the coronation of Queen Elizabeth II which took place on 2 June 1953. The pub stood on the corner of Chapel Street and was demolished around 1970. (W. Butler & Co., L4/BRO/I/1)

Silas Caddick, tobacconist and newsagent in Oxford Street in the 1950s. (*Wolverhampton Chronicle*, L3/CAD/I/1)

Bilston Post Office workers, *c.*1922, wearing their medals from the First World War. The staff in the front row are mainly counter clerks and the others are mainly postmen. The young man at the front was one of two messengers, in the second row, fifth from left is Mr Lines, sixth from left is Mr Ryan. In the third row, second from left is Mr Shorthouse who lived over the post office in Hall Street, fifth from left is Mr Parkes. (Miss M. Lines, K1/BIL/E/3)

Councillors and officers of Bilston Borough Council on 28 March 1966, only a few days before Bilston merged with Wolverhampton. In the centre is Bilston's 31st and last Mayor, Councillor Harold Aubrey Humphries. Bilston Council consisted of five Aldermen and fifteen councillors.

The Council Chamber at Bilston Town Hall. (*Dudley Herald*)

Hickman Park was opened on 17 June 1911. Musicians wishing to play at the bandstand had to apply to the Council for permission as one of the bylaws prohibited singing and the playing of instruments in the park.

A guide book dated 1961 states that the park consisted of twelve acres of well-timbered grounds, laid out with lawns, flower-beds and a rose-garden. Council bylaws prohibited the picking of buds, blossoms, flowers or leaves.

Public tennis courts were also available at Hickman Park. The playing of games such as tennis, cricket, bowls, quoits, rounders and archery was not permitted, except in certain designated areas of the park.

The opening of the Sons of Rest pavilion in Hickman Park by Bob Edwards MP on 8 December 1955. (*Dudley Herald*)

The opening of Bilston Public Library and Reading Room on 18 March 1937 by Alderman T.R. Wood. The building, Brueton House, was purchased by the council in 1935 and enlarged over the next two years. Extensions were also made for a museum and art gallery, opened at the same time as the library. There were approximately 45,000 books available free of charge to Bilston residents or anyone holding a library ticket from another authority. Non-residents who did not possess a library ticket had to pay an annual subscription of 5/-. (Z4/BIL/E/6)

The Reading Room at Bilston Library showing the newspaper stands. (Z4/BIL/NEW/4)

These two photographs show a Midland Red single-decker bus being fitted out for use as a mobile library in 1960. A guidebook for 1964 states that the mobile library carries nearly 2,000 books for all classes of readers to housing estates situated towards the outskirts of town. An article in the *Bilston & Willenhall Times* in May 1964 reported that the converted bus was suffering from engine failure and the mobile service which had operated from Tuesday-Friday had to cease temporarily. (*Midland Red/Express & Star*, Z5/BIL/1, Z5/BIL/2)

Remembrance Day, 11 November 1956. The town hall is on the left and in the procession were the mayor and mayoress, Councillor and Mrs W.H. Sandland, councillors and officials, Bob Edwards MP and representatives of the British Legion, RAFA, scouts, guides, boys' and girls' brigades and the police. The service was held at St Leonard's church. (*Dudley Herald*)

Remembrance day at Bilston War Memorial. On 11 November 1921 three war memorials were unveiled in the Bilston area: one at Ettingshall, one at Bradley and this one at Swan Bank, Bilston. Built of Portland stone by Messrs Dove & Co. of London, the cross was designed by Sir Reginald Blomfield. The central memorial for the township of Bilston was, however, an ex-servicemen's club and recreation ground at the Laburnums. Fifty-nine awards were also made to local men who had gained distinction in the war.

Two
Tettenhall

Old Hill showing the Rock Hotel, *c*.1920. (C1/OLDH/8/2)

Tettenhall, that 'sweet, peaceful place' where

Hampton's sons in vacant hours repair
Taste rural joys, and breath a purer air

according to Revd J. Ferneyhough in 1789. The ancient village of Tettenhall, mentioned in the Domesday Book, is situated 21½ miles north-west of Wolverhampton at a height of between 300-500 feet above sea level. The village developed around the two centres of Upper and Lower Green, separated by the sandstone Tettenhall ridge. Lower Green is probably the older of the two settlements and may be the green mentioned in 1327 when Thomas in the Green was a tenant.

Settlement spread from these two centres and by the early seventeenth century there were houses in Old Hill, where the main road climbed the ridge before a cutting through the Rock was made in the early 1820s. During the nineteenth century the village grew as a residential area with large houses such as Danes Court in Stockwell End and Woodthorne in Wergs Road being built in the 1860s. Splendid villas began to appear along the Wergs Road, mostly inhabited by businessmen who had made their money out of Black Country industry and now wanted to move out into the countryside.

Many smaller houses were also built at Stockwell End and terraces were built in Limes Road, Regis Road and Nursery Walk in the 1870s-1890s. In contrast to the large houses occupied by wealthy landowners, the workers' cottages of the last century were often draughty, damp and sparsely furnished and in 1892 only a third of houses in the village had running water.

After the First World War council housing was built around Regis Road followed by further building in the area during the 1950s and 60s, some of which was to house 'overspill' from Wolverhampton which was struggling to house its own expanding population. Private housing developments have also taken place since the two world wars and the character of the whole area has become largely residential during the last hundred years, especially attracting business people working in Wolverhampton. By 1931 the population of Tettenhall was 4,691, increasing to 15,400 by around 1964.

Industry in the area has mostly been limited to agriculture, in addition to quarrying and a few cottage industries such as nailing and lockmaking. Arable and dairy farming were important and by the late eighteenth century Tettenhall Wood was described as an excellent sheep walk, with the sheep bred there being 'of good size and producing fine wool'. Pig keeping was also common and in the late eighteenth century pigs were allowed to feed on the large quantities of fallen pears in the parish. In 1796 it was said that 'many hundreds' of Tettenhall Pear trees grew in the parish. The pear, also called the Tettenhall Dick, was described in the *Gardeners' Chronicle* of 1841 as 'worthless' although it was supplied to local markets and taken by canal as far as Lancashire. There are some Tettenhall Pear trees in the area today and the fruit is mostly used in cooking.

Sand quarrying was carried out at Compton, Wightwick and near Tettenhall village, with some pits still being worked until the early twentieth century. Metal working went on in the parish from the late sixteenth century and over the next three hundred years products made included hinges, buckles, toys, rings, swivels, keys, nails, spectacle-frames and watch-chains. By the late 1700s, lockmaking had become the chief trade and large numbers of locksmiths settled in Tettenhall Wood after the enclosure of the common in 1809. By 1841 there were fifty five lockmakers in the parish with thirty one of them living at Tettenhall Wood and the others around the areas of Compton, Finchfield and Lower Street.

The abundance of picture postcards of Tettenhall testifies to its place as a tourist destination for the inhabitants of neighbouring Wolverhampton. Frequently described as picturesque, it remains so today with its two greens and leafy aspect. Still referred to as 'the village' by locals, Tettenhall has retained its village atmosphere depite the fears that it would be overwhelmed by its larger neighbour.

RESPICE · ASPICE PROSPICE

The arms are vert on a chevron engrailed between three trees eradicated or as many fountains and the crest is on a wreath of the colours, upon a mount vert in front of a windmill argent two battle-axes in saltire gules. The trees are meant to represent the three great Royal forests in the area, the battle-axes refer to the battle of Tettenhall in 910 and the round discs or 'fountains' represent Tettenhall Pool and the two streams in the parish. The windmill recalls the corn mills in the area. The background colour of the shield is green (altered from the original suggestion of blue) and divided by the chevron to represent Upper and Lower Green. The motto *Respice, aspice, prospice* means 'look back, look around, look forward' and was chosen from a number of alternatives suggested by Gerald P. Mander. Some of his suggestions show concern for the continued independence of Tettenhall from Wolverhampton e.g. *Mihi solicitudo futuri* (I fear for the future), *Semper floreat* (Let it flourish forever). Granted in 1938 at a cost of £81 10s 0 and paid for by subscription, the design of the coat of arms owes much to local historian Gerald P. Mander whose correspondence with Tettenhall UDC on the subject is preserved in Wolverhampton Archives & Local Studies.

Upper Green from Wrottesley Road in the early twentieth century. A Lorain tram can be seen on the Wergs Road and in the centre, between the trees, can just be seen the Victorian water fountain. This has stood here since 1890 and over the years has become blackened with fumes from the heavy traffic on the Wergs Road. (A2/UPP/2)

The Rock and Upper Green, probably around the turn of the century. Upper Green was known as Marsh Green in the early eighteenth century but the name Upper Green was coming into use by 1780. (A2/UPP/20)

The blacksmith's forge on Upper Green at the junction of Stockwell Road and Clifton Road. The Southwick family were blacksmiths in Tettenhall for many years with Henry Southwick being listed in trade directories 1834-1860 and James Southwick 1872-1892. (A2/UPP/30)

A view of Upper Green in the 1950s with the Post Office just visible through the trees. In February 1990 a lime tree near the clock tower which was thought to be at least 150 years old was uprooted by 90mph gales. (A2/UPP/14)

Tettenhall Road and Upper Green looking towards the Rock, probably in the 1930s. Note the trolley bus poles on the left. Trolley buses began running to Tettenhall on 1 January 1929 and continued until 30 June 1963. The *Express & Star* of 19 April 1961 shows an artist's impression of a proposed pedestrian bridge which would have crossed the Rock at the top of the cutting by the second trolley bus pole. (M.Wheeler, C2/TETT/8/1)

An early twentieth-century view looking up the Rock with a Lorain tram just passing Avenue House Lodge on the right. Rock House and Old Hill are on the left. The cutting through the Rock was made between 1820 and 1823, although not by Thomas Telford as is often thought. Telford first suggested re-routing the road through Aldersley and then came up with the idea of a short, rising tunnel. Both of these were rejected by the trustees of the road and so Telford declined to undertake the supervision of the cutting. (Alex Chatwin, C2/TETT/7/3)

Upper Street looking towards Old Hill, probably in the late nineteenth century, showing the raised pavement and railings still remembered with affection by many local people. On the right is the Rose & Crown inn. The area was redeveloped with flats in the 1950s. (M. Lines, C1/UPT/8/1)

The Rose & Crown inn, Upper Street in 1913, looking towards Upper Green. According to Webb's Almanack 1892, it was the custom during the Michaelmas Wake celebrations to tie a cord from the upper windows of the Rose & Crown to the opposite side of the hill. On this cord would be suspended ducks, geese, turkeys and other poultry and then local men and youths would be blindfolded, placed on donkeys and ponies and sent down the hill. Anything they could drag off the line as they rode underneath would remain their property. (C1/UPT/7/2)

A wintry view of Church Road looking towards the Rock, with Lower Green on the left and Rock House in the distance. The cottage on the corner still remains and the scene looks little different today. (C2/CHURC/5/3)

Church Road and Lower Green looking towards the church of St Michael and All Angels. The cottages on the left have now gone. (A2/LOWE/2)

Crowther Road with St Michael's Church visible through the trees, a reminder that Tettenhall was once protected by extensive forests. (C2/CROW/4/1)

Lower Street in 1913, from the junction with the Rock. The road rises very steeply up to the Rock here and from Henwood Road on the other side as a result of the cutting through of the Rock in the 1820s. In order to make a more gentle gradient for the Tettenhall Road on its way through the Rock, the spoil from the cutting was taken further down the hill to make a ramp. The natural level of the road here is indicated by Lower Green. (C1/LOW/6/4)

The Smestow Valley from Newbridge showing one of the platforms at Tettenhall station (extreme right). The station opened on 11 May 1925 and the last passenger train on the line ran on 31 October 1932. The line remained open for goods traffic until 1964 and the track was lifted in 1967-8. The railway bed was acquired by Wolverhampton Council in 1974 and renamed Valley Park. (K3/TET/E/3)

Meadow View Terrace was cut in half during the construction of the Wolverhampton and Kingswinford Railway which began in 1913 and finished in 1924 (including a break of about four years during the First World War). The houses were built sometime between 1885 and 1902. Three houses were demolished to make way for the railway. (C1/MEAD/8/1)

Compton Mill Pool in Henwood Lane. Compton mill stood at the Compton end of the road and is believed to be one of the mills mentioned in 1249 as forming part of the royal manor of Tettenhall. Described in 1743 as a corn or blade mill, it was apparently used as a flour mill for much of the nineteenth century but had gone out of use by the early 1900s and the pool had been drained by 1919. (B6/COM/2)

A postcard of Henwood Lane which is postmarked 1907 although the road is marked as Henwood Road on an Ordnance Survey map of 1902. The name seems to come from an open field called Henwood which was mentioned in 1517. Part of the field had been enclosed by the early eighteenth century but the other part of the field was still open-field arable in 1710 and was known as Lower Henwood. (Olive Beddoe, C2/HEN/0/3)

Compton Road in the early 1900s showing the entrance to Compton Coal Wharf on the right. The sign advertises the retail and wholesale of 'best Cannock Chase and other coals' by the proprietor Leonard T. Law. The yard is now used by a boat builder. (C2/COM/6/1)

Compton Road looking towards Tettenhall in October 1921. The clear marking of the boundaries was probably connected with the proposed Wolverhampton Borough extension of 1921 which, if it had been approved, would have seen the incorporation into Wolverhampton of much of the area which came into the borough in 1966. (C2/COM/7/8)

A postcard view of Compton Road, postmarked 1922. On the left is the Oddfellows Hall, demolished around 1937. The present building was extensively refurbished in 1988. (Brian Perry, C2/COM/6/3)

Compton Holloway, probably around the turn of the century. There is evidence that sand was dug at the bottom of the Holloway, probably by the mid 1830s, the sand being used for iron foundries and for making mortar. (C2/COMP/5/8)

Tettenhall Wood Institute and Wood Road. Webb's Almanac of 1905 describes the Working Men's Institute, established in 1887 and moving into this building in 1893, as being on Minge Way Corner, Tettenhall Wood. Persons over eighteen were eligible to become members and enjoy the facilities of reading room, bagatelle and smoke room, lending library, bowling green, bowling alley and air gun club. (M6/TWO/E/1)

Wood Road, c. 1929. Wood Road, Mount Road, the southern end of School Road and the northern end of Church Road all date from the enclosure in 1809 of most of Tettenhall Wood common, formerly Kingsley Wood. A petition for the enclosure of the common described it as the haunt of 'gypsies, thieves and other disreputable people'. (Mrs J. Turner, C2/WOO/0/3)

Cornwall Road from the late 1950s/early 1960s. This street, called 'a prize-winning council development' in the Council's 1960 guidebook, was given its name by Tettenhall UDC at a meeting on 26 March 1956 and was part of an extensive post-war building programme. Three estates were built, Long Lake immediately after the war, Woodhouse in the late 1940s/early 1950s and the Grange in the mid-1950s. Between 1945 and 1955 Tettenhall UDC completed the building of 650 dwellings. Some of the dwellings were reserved for people on the Council's own waiting list, whilst others were allocated as 'overspill' for tenants from Wolverhampton and Bilston where space for new council housing was in short supply. Wolverhampton also had overspill agreements with Wednesfield and Seisdon councils.

Culverting the Smestow brook at Aldersley Stadium on 12 September 1955. The work is being carried out by the firm of Greenley Bros. Tettenhall lies on the watershed between the Smestow brook flowing south and the Penk flowing north towards the Trent. The Smestow rises in Bushbury and enters Tettenhall at Aldersley, flowing south towards the Stour and the Severn. The goddess of the River Severn is Sabrina and this is apparently the origin of the name Sabrina Road which is near to the Smestow in Wightwick. (B5/SME/7)

The junction of the Smestow and Graiseley brooks with Henwood Road to the left. A tributary of the Smestow, Graiseley brook formed the boundary between Tettenhall and Wolverhampton east of Compton. The photograph is supposed to show a tip which may be on the left, close to the site of the mill race and pool from Compton mill. It is difficult to date the view although it is certainly pre-World War Two. (Bennett Clark, B5/SME/4)

Wergs Road, probably around the turn of the century. The Wergs was inhabited by 1304 and lies on the Shrewsbury road, north-west of Tettenhall. The name means willows, presumably after those growing alongside the Penk which flows through the area. (C2/WERG/0/1)

There was a Crown inn on the north side of the Wergs Road by 1834. This picture is from a sale catalogue of 1907 which describes the pub as recently-built and including a smoke room and bar, tap room with serving window, pantry and scullery, four bedrooms, stable, loose-box cow house and piggery. The house and land of four acres was let to Mr H.J. Bradley on a 21-year lease from September 1905 at a rental of £50 per annum. (DX/132/1)

Wergs Hall, was listed as a family mansion in the 1907 sale catalogue, built in the Italian style with terraces on the principal fronts, artistically laid out pleasure grounds and gardens, dells, grottos, ferneries and a fine ornamental lake covering several acres. The 167 acre estate was sold following the death of its owner Miss Helen Perry who had lived there since the death in 1885 of her brother, T.J. Perry, a Bilston ironmaster, who purchased the hall in 1872. In 1963 the hall was bought by Sir Alfred McAlpine & Son Ltd. (N2/WER/E/1)

The Drawing Room at Wergs Hall, taken from the 1907 sale catalogue of the Wergs Estate. The room was heated by a special hot-water apparatus and boasted chimney pieces of marble or mahogany and walnut with dog and other grates with brass and copper mountings. In addition, the drawing room, dining room and library all had Scagliola marble columns in relief. (DX/132/1)

Also taken from the 1907 sale catalogue, this is the gardener's house, nearly opposite the front gates of the Hall. It was described as a well-built Gothic structure with two sitting rooms, kitchen, three bedrooms and pantry with enclosed yard. (DX/132/1)

From the same catalogue comes this picture of the Wergs Post Office, part of a lot of four cottages fronting the Holyhead road (i.e. Wergs Road) which were said to have large, productive gardens and well and pump for water supply. (DX/132/1)

Tettenhall Towers on 12 July 1897. In the top row, from left to right are: Mr Ernest Fowler, Mr Hamo Douglas Thorneycroft, Miss Florence Thorneycroft, Miss Dorothy Thorneycroft, Mr Beach, Miss Eleanor Thorneycroft, Miss Edith Fowler, Miss Minnie Walker, Mr G.B. Thorneycroft, Mrs T. Thorneycroft, Master Mervyn Thorneycroft, Lady Hickman, Lieut-Col. Thomas Thorneycroft, Mrs G.B. Thorneycroft and Mrs Lees. In the bottom row are friends and neighbours from Tettenhall Parish. The house was built by 1763 for Thomas Pearson and described as Grecian in style. The two polygonal towers were added in 1866 and they originally ended in balustrades as the lodge still does. Born in Willenhall in 1822, the son of G.B. Thorneycroft, a Black Country ironmaster, Thomas Thorneycroft attended Wolverhampton Grammar School and ran the ironworks for some twenty six years after his father's death until the works and collieries were closed in 1877. After this, he concentrated on the many properties he owned or leased, notably Tettenhall Towers.

Col. Thorneycroft bought Tettenhall Towers in 1854 having been a tenant there since 1851. By 1880 he had added this private theatre with 500 seats and special effects, including a stage with a giant 44 ft cascade of water over which coloured lights played. After a performance the water was then used to thoroughly flush out the drains, drainage being a subject in which the colonel was very interested!

The Great Hall at Tettenhall Towers. Heavy panelling and carved woodwork were a feature of the house's decoration, together with various trophies of wild animals. (N2/TET/I/2)

Gorsty Hayes cottage in Haywood Drive was also owned by Col. Thorneycroft who carried out some restoration work on the building. The half-timbered cottage seems to date from the seventeenth century and is believed to have been a forester's lodge. Local tradition has it that Henry II once spent some days hunting in the area. The building was bought by the Roman Catholic church in 1962 for use as a presbytery for the adjacent church of St Thomas of Canterbury.

The dining room at Gorsty Hayes in the late nineteenth century.

The timber-framed Wightwick Manor was designed by Edward Ould of the Liverpool firm Grayson & Ould and built for Theodore Mander in 1887 with additions in 1893. Ould was a specialist in half-timbered buildings and was much influenced by Tudor architecture. The lodge and barn adjoining the manor date from the late sixteenth or early seventeenth century although they have been heavily restored by Ould. The chief glory of the house lies in its furnishings and decoration which, like the house itself, are Victorian but hark back to an ideal past. Theodore Mander decorated the house under the influence of Morris and Ruskin and the collection was much augmented by Sir Geoffrey and Lady Mander who decided in 1935 that the house should be preserved as a period piece. The house was given to the National Trust in 1937. (N1/WIG/E/2)

This picture of the Grove, Wood Road shows it as it was rebuilt after the war. During the Second World War the house, then the home of the Pratt family, received a direct hit from a lone German plane jettisoning its bombs. Rebuilding could not take place until after the war so the family moved elsewhere and the property was sold to Harold Fulwood who had the house rebuilt, and moved in, around 1946. This house was in its turn demolished and is now the site of Maythorn Gardens. (Mrs E.M. Gamston, N3/GRO/E/1a)

Tettenhall Wood House stood near the end of the present Grange Road and was built in 1835 for Theodosia Hinckes who inherited around 390 acres of land in Tettenhall from her father Revd Josiah Hinckes. The castellated Gothic villa was designed by Thomas Rickman and by 1915 had passed to V.E. Hickman, a younger son of Sir Alfred Hickman. Tettenhall UDC bought 24 acres of the estate in 1946 and built a housing estate there, buying an additional 51 acres in 1953. At the same time the council took out an option on the house and a further 16 acres when Mrs Ethel Hickman died or left. She died in 1969 at the age of 103 and the house and land passed to Wolverhampton Corporation, the successor to the UDC. It was subsequently demolished and private houses and a school are now on the site. (N3/TETT/E/1)

The Grange, just off the Wergs Road. Not to be confused with the house of the same name in Grange Road, Tettenhall, this house overlooks Wrottesley Park and was described in a 1924 sale catalogue as 'one of the choicest residential properties of the district'. It was built in 1863 and amongst its rooms had five principal bedrooms, three second bedrooms, two maids' bedrooms and three excellent cellars. (N3/GRA/E/1)

The Manor House, Upper Green, situated on the green between Regis Road and Limes Road. Flats now stand on the site. (N1/MAN/E/1)

Both of these photographs date from around 1920 and show Compton Farm, Compton Road which belonged to the Wheeler family for many years until it was sold in 1925. Crops mentioned in the diary of Sarah Ann Wheeler written in the early 1890s include wheat, barley, swedes, turnips, parsnips, potatoes, sprouts, carrots, cabbage, kidney beans and celery. She also talks about churning butter, preparing produce for market, plucking ducks, holding down pigs to be killed and helping her mother to make pork pies. (M. Wheeler, L8/COM/7, L8/COM/6)

Upper Green farm, Tettenhall before the village pond was turned into a paddling pool in the 1930s. (Brian Perry, L8/UPP/E/1)

The Old Smithy photographed on 10 March 1913. Together with the Forge Cottages, this building stood on the corner of Clifton Road and Stockwell Road and was demolished sometime before 1919. (L8/TET/E/1)

Wynn's general store on the corner of High Street and Upper Green. Sarah Wynn, standing in the doorway, started the shop around 1865. It was later taken over by her son David who introduced a bakery and built a bakehouse at the rear. The shop was also a post office. (Mr D.J. Wynn, L3/WYN/E/1)

Hall's dispensing chemist and mineral water company, 291-293 Tettenhall Road c. 1930. (L3/HALC/E/1)

Chas. F. Weaver's Newbridge Coal Wharf and the Staffordshire & Worcestershire canal, c. 1910. In a 1912 advertisement the company offered Cannock and Rugeley House Coal, Works Coal, Gas Coke, Foundry Coke and Breezes in small or large quantities. (L6/WEAV/E/1)

A view of Joseph Walker's coal wharf at Compton from a postcard postmarked 1908. (Olive Beddoe, D7/STA/49)

Compton Road, showing the Boat Inn, looking towards Compton. The building is lower than road level owing to road improvements which increased the height of the road. The Boat stood opposite the high wall next to the junction with Compton Hill Drive. (L4/BOA/E/2)

The Boat Inn pictured in 1926. The lady on the left is Mrs Webberley holding her son, Frank, the little girl is her daughter, Wendy, and the other two ladies are Nell and Jean Colligan. The licensee at the time was John Colligan. (Frank Webberley/Olive Beddoe, L4/BOA/E/3)

A carol service in the Pilot, Aldersley, c. 1954. (Butler's magazine, April 1955, L4/PIL/I/1)

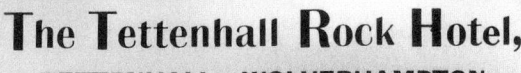

The Rock Hotel, Old Hill, Tettenhall. Previously called the Rose & Crown, by 1814 the pub had become the Old Rose & Crown and appears in trade directories under this name until about 1892. The grounds were opened in 1843 as Rock Villa pleasure gardens and boasted a bowling green and bandstand. In the summer months and at holiday times there would be fireworks and occasionally balloon ascents. (L4/ROC/E/4)

The Tettenhall Rock Hotel,

TETTENHALL, WOLVERHAMPTON.

THE FINEST VIEW IN THE MIDLANDS.
CLOSE TO THE ELECTRIC TRAMS.

Wines and Spirits of the choicest quality.

BOWLING GREEN.   **BILLIARDS.**

ARTHUR LAMSDALE, Proprietor.

Tettenhall golf course, from a postcard. The South Staffordshire Golf Club has been in Tettenhall since its move from Penn Common in 1908 to the site of former farm land at Stockwell End. (M. Wheeler, M2/TET/1)

The paddling pool on Upper Green was opened, c. 1934. It was previously a farm pool and appears on a map of 1613. The Graham family of the *Express & Star* paid for the conversion of the pool and an article in the newspaper on 19 October 1933 contains a photograph of the drained pool awaiting the fixing of concrete sides and bed prior to opening the following summer. (M1/TET/1)

Singing practice with Miss Daphne at Christ Church Junior School, School Road, Tettenhall Wood, c. 1965. The school pianist, Mrs Sherwood, is playing piano. The building in School Road opened in 1874 and the Junior School was on this site until it moved to new premises in Woodcote Road in 1974. The School Road building is now home to Tettenhall Wood Special School. (Brenda Swatman, Y5/CHRI/9)

Christ Church, Tettenhall Wood was consecrated on 29 September 1866, although it originated in a mission established from St Michael's in 1844 in the infants' schoolroom. The church, made of Codsall stone, was designed in a decorated Gothic style by Bateman & Corser of Birmingham, following a limited competition amongst local architects. The cost of the church was met largely by voluntary contributions with an endowment of £100 per year from Lord Wrottesley. (G. Smith, E1/CH/I/1)

The VAD Hospital at the old Manor House, Old Hill, Tettenhall. Probably taken around the end of the First World War, the VAD (Voluntary Aid Detachment) nurses can be seen in the doorway. The building, formerly Tettenhall vicarage, was demolished in the 1950s. (J1/VAD/E/1)

Wolverhampton and district repatriated prisoners of war visiting the Red Cross and St John Hospital at the Manor House, Upper Green on 11 November 1943. The *Express & Star* of the following day reported that the men watched volunteer workers making bandages and garments for use in hospitals and for shipment abroad. The repatriated men were: Corporal Rhodes, Lance-Corporal G. Aspray, Driver A.C. Powis and Privates W.E. Price, S. Doughty, B. Eastelow, H. Jones, W. Slater, G. Kirkbride and W. Hill. (Mrs Beeston, Y1/PRI/1)

CORONATION MEMORIAL. TETTENHALL. 1911.

The unveiling of the coronation memorial tower and clock, Upper Green on 22 June 1911. The tower was designed by F.T. Beck of Darlington Street, built by Mr Cave of Wolverhampton and the clock was supplied by John Smith & Sons of Derby. The 21ft high, 5ft wide tower is built of Darley Dale stone and rests on a 12ft square platform of Yorkshire stone. The tower and clock were presented to Tettenhall as a permanent memorial of the coronation of George V by Mr and Mrs Edward Swindley. There is an inscription on each side of the tower: 'I labour here with all my might to tell the hour by day and night; for every hour that passes there is a record; for every hour that strikes there is a joy; for every hour that comes there is a hope'. (V2/GEOV/5)

The Tettenhall Coaching and Driving Club, Upper Green, *c*. 1897. Formed in 1883 by Lieut. Colonel Thorneycroft, the club met at West Park every Saturday afternoon in the summer months, after which they generally drove to Chillington Pool. This picture may be from the opening of the season on 9 August 1897 when the Driving Club met at Tettenhall Green before travelling to the Crown Hotel, Albrighton for tea and an hour's music with a few songs. In the first coach are: Lieut. Colonel Thorneycroft, Capt. Thorneycroft, Mr and Mrs Barker, Mrs and Miss Burnett, Mr Butler and Mrs Chub. In the second coach are the Mayor and Mayoress and party. In the third are Mr and Mrs Podmore, Miss Florence Thorneycroft, General Hadow, Mr and Mrs Taylor. In the fourth, Mr G.B. Thorneycroft, Mr W.R. Smith, Mr T.B. Cope, Miss Eleanor Thorneycroft and at the rear is Col. Thorneycroft's waggon with the band and party. (A2/UPP/31)

Three
Wednesfield

The Canal at Wednesfield, Staffs.

Wednesfield viewed from the Wyrley and Essington canal with the tower of St Thomas' church clearly visible in the centre background and Pinfold bridge on the right. (D7/WYR/WED/3)

Wednesfield lies two miles to the north east of Wolverhampton and has a history stretching back to at least 910 when a battle between the Saxons and the Danes took place in this area. The exact location is unknown and the battle could have ranged over quite a large area including both Wednesfield and Tettenhall. Certainly the first recorded name, 'Wodnesfelde' is Anglo Saxon in origin deriving from the Norse god of war, Woden, and reinforcing the connection with the battle.

In 994 Lady Wulfrun granted land for the upkeep of the monastery at Heantun which included land at Wodnesfelde. Wulfruna's Heantun eventually became Wolverhampton and by the time of Domesday the clerks of Heantun held five hides of land in Wodnesfelde.

During the later Middle Ages, when the forests were being cleared, a number of moated halls and homesteads were built in this part of South Staffordshire. By the eighteenth century many of them had been rebuilt, outside the original moats, as substantial farmhouses such as those at Long Knowle, Prestwood and Ashmore Park.

By 1741 the township of Wednesfield covered a large area including many villages and hamlets such as Wednesfield Heath (now Heath Town), Wood End, Neachells and Moseley. There was no parish church for these communities and people had to travel to St Peter's in Wolverhampton. An Act of Parliament was needed before a church could be built and the preamble begins; 'Whereas the township or hamlet of Wednesfield ... is a large and populous place, inhabited chiefly by persons employed in the Iron Manufactures ... land whereas the Parish or Mother Church is near two miles distant and the highway between ... being very deep and dirty in the Winter Season, it is very inconvenient and troublesome to the Inhabitants of ... Wednesfield to attend Divine Service ...' The church was built in 1750 on the village green and dedicated to St Thomas. Wednesfield did not become an independent parish until 1849.

The cholera epidemic of 1832, which decimated the population in nearby places such as Bilston, seems to have had little impact in Wednesfield. White's Directory of 1834 reports only one recorded case and no deaths from a population of 1,879. The Cholera Commission of 1848 stated that '... in Wednesfield there were no sewers or drains whatsoever, and the place abounded with nuisances. The streets were unpaved and there were no public lights at all. The water supply was unsafe, but the death rate was not so high as in Wolverhampton or Bilston'.

Nineteenth-century maps show that most of the land was being used for agriculture although there was mining at Ashmore Park and Wednesfield Heath. There was no resident Squire or Lord of the Manor and the people were mainly employed in making metal goods, including locks, keys and traps, in small workshops in their homes or backyards. In the 1860s there was no power driven machinery or workshop employing more than nine persons. John Smallshire, a local historian, has described Wednesfield at that time as 'a small community of ill-paid individualists ...'.

When the church was built meetings were held in the vestry and officials appointed to run parish affairs. In 1856 a Joint Sanitary Committee was formed with Wednesfield Heath, the first form of local government. This became a Joint Local Board in 1863 and in 1893 Wednesfield and Heath Town both became Urban District Councils. In 1927 Heath Town became part of Wolverhampton.

In 1931 the population of Wednesfield was 9,106 and by 1951 had risen to 17, 400. New housing estates were built 'over Ward's bridge' to the north of the village centre under the 'Overspill' agreement of 1952 and the population was around 23,500 by 1956. One resident who moved to the Moat House estate in the early 1950s describes how rural the scene was and how the few shops in the village 'were unhurried about their opening times'.

Wednesfield's Official Guide for 1956 reported the threat of amalgamation stating that 'Wednesfield has always kept its separate social and communal life, which is precious to it. It has a sturdy independence, a strong sense of civic pride and a belief in the ability of its own people to look after its own affairs.' However, reading articles in the local press from the time, there is a feeling that change was inevitable and that, unlike 910, this was a battle that was not going to be won.

The Armorial Bearings of
WEDNESFIELD URBAN DISTRICT COUNCIL

The Wednesfield coat of arms was granted to Wednesfield Urban District Council on 20th May 1965. The description of the blazon is 'per chevron sable and gules in chief two double warded keys wards upward and in a base a saxon crown or on a chief or two barrulets azure surmounted of mural crown gules'. The crest description is 'issuant from a saxon crown or a mount vert thereon a raven sable wings addorsed and transfixed in bend by a spear head downward gules.' The mantling is sable and is doubled or. The motto means 'Wednesfield Forever' and appears to have been a late show of defiance against being absorbed by Wolverhampton. The keys are a reference to one of Wednesfield's most important trades, keymaking. The Saxon crown on a red background represents the battle between the Saxons and the Danes. Wednesfield had previously attempted to adopt a coat of arms in 1956 but had decided against it as the College of Arms were unwilling to include the Wednesfield seal which depicted the battle in pictorial form. The proposed design included the Saxon crown and keys but the motto would have been *Post proelium securitas* (After the battle, security).

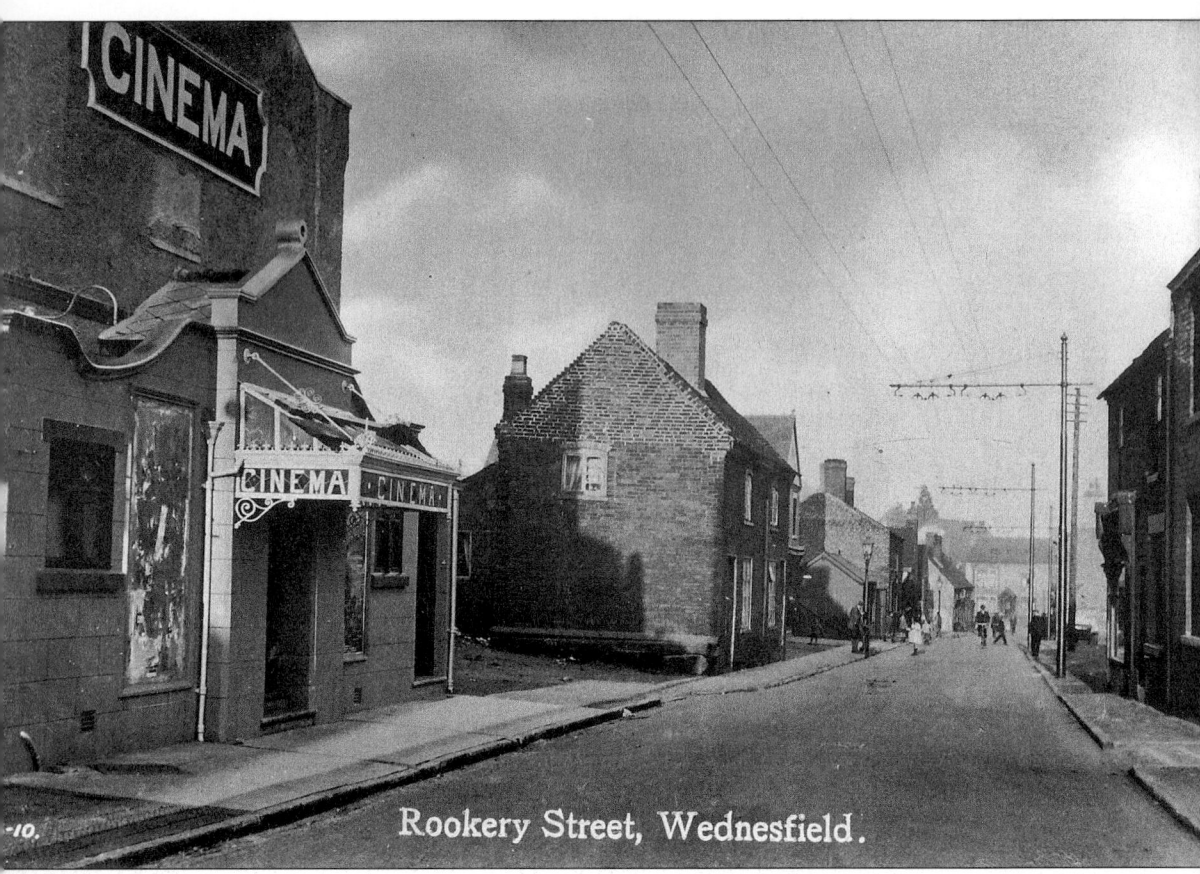

Rookery Street, Wednesfield.

Rookery Street showing the cinema which was known locally as the 'Smack'. Local legend explains this nickname as deriving from the sound of cinemagoers smacking the fleas that lived in the upholstery! The cinema was actually named the 'Ideal' and the photograph probably dates from the end of the 1930s when the porch was added. The last film was shown around 1957 and the building was used as a carpet warehouse until 1991 when it burned down.

Rookery Street looking towards the High Street. Alfred Squires Hardware Stores is clearly visible on the right hand side. Thomas Squire, a lockmaker, started a business supplying iron and steel strips and wires in 1866. In 1896 his nephew Alfred took over the business and was joined by his brother Henry. In 1933 they acquired a wholesale and retail ironmongery shop in Rookery Street which was managed by Alfred's son Cyril in the 1950s. An advertisement in the 1950 edition of Wednesfield Official Guide describes it as supplying 'Everything in Hardware for the Home and Garden'. The presence of trolley bus wires indicates that the photograph is later than 1923 and the motor vehicles suggest the 1930s.

Well Lane looking towards Church Street photographed between 1902 and 1919. The building on the right is the Sunday school attached to the Wesleyan Chapel which stood further to the right. It is now used as a Sikh Temple. The buildings on the left are on the corner of Rookery Street and Church Street. Part of this block still stands; some of the oldest buildings remaining in this part of Wednesfield.

Wednesfield High Street in 1959 showing the Regal cinema on the right. This cinema, opened in 1935 and closed in 1962, was always considered a more upmarket establishment than the 'Smack' The site is now occupied by a supermarket. On the left you can see some older buildings and evidence of construction work. The tree on the right stands in the corner of St Thomas' churchyard. (C1/HIGH/7/1)

Wednesfield, Staffs.

The High Street in 1959 looking towards Lichfield Road. This view was taken from the same corner of St Thomas' churchyard visible in the previous photograph and shows how narrow the High Street was with nineteenth-century buildings on both sides. As the 'Overspill' housing programme was well under way by this time traffic was increasing and it was decided to demolish all of the properties on the right hand side of the road and rebuild new shops further back. This allowed the widening of the road and provision of parking places. Traffic congestion however has continued to be a problem to the present day although it should be alleviated by the imminent opening of a new bypass. (C1/HIGH/8/12)

A much older view of the High Street looking towards the church. The building on the extreme left is part of the Dog and Partridge public house which is still in existence. The Gregory family took over the pub around 1879 and kept it for more than eighty years. This view dates from the beginning of the century before they carried out alterations. The building is shown on the 1843 tithe map. The apparently casual photograph may actually have been carefully posed with boys in school clothes occupying the foreground.

Alfred Squire Road showing the council offices on the left. The council offices were opened on the 2 April 1955 in Regal Fields. The previous council offices had been in the High Street. The road was constructed in 1965 and named after Alfred Squire who as well as being the owner of Thomas Squire & Co and Squire's Hardware was postmaster for many years, a member of Wednesfield UDC and a leading member of the Methodist Church. Cyril Squire, his son, was Chairman of the UDC in 1955-1956. (C2/ALFR/5/1)

Pickering Road in the early 1960s with Lathe House under construction. Pickering Road first appears on Wednesfield street maps in 1961 and may have been named after Fred Pickering a local builder. Three blocks of nine storey flats including Lathe House were built in Lakefield Road in 1962 and occupied by 1965. (C2/PIC/0/1)

Ridge Lane showing council housing built in the inter-war period. The lane itself is clearly marked on maps going back to the 1880s and may have formed part of an ancient route through the parish but the housing was built in the 1930s. This photograph would appear to have been taken when the development was quite new. (C2/RIDG/1)

Woden Avenue in 1959 with Woden Avenue School, now known as Wodensfield School on the left. Another area that was developed for council housing between the two world wars lay to the west of Amos Lane including Nordley Hill, Vicarage Road, Victoria Road and Woden Avenue. The school was opened in 1932. (C2/WOD/6/1)

Prestwood Road pictured before 1939. This view gives an idea of how the area looked before the large scale housing development which took place in the 1950s. The photograph was taken looking towards Wood End Road. The cottage was a smithy kept by Elijah Edwards and the house belonged to Mr Wheeler who was a fruiterer. They were demolished around 1952-54. (Mrs Boyden, C2/PRES/0/4)

Bradburn Road in 1959 showing a block of three story flats in the background. The Long Knowle Estate was one of the first estates built to the north of Wednesfield in response to the post-war housing shortage and 'Overspill' agreement. The estate took its name from an ancient farmstead, originally, Long Noles or Nowel. The house was demolished in 1935 and the ancient timber reused in a 'tudor' house near Compton. Most of the roads on the estate were named after local people including council members. (C2/BRAD/8/1)

Moathouse Lane in 1959 showing the Moathouse Estate shopping centre. Moathouse Farm was another ancient moated farmstead. The original building stood near to the Moathouse bridge over the canal but was replaced by a new building in 1860 which was constructed close to Lichfield Road. This building was known as Hyde's Farm when it was demolished prior to the construction of the estate in the mid 1950s. (C2/MOA/1/1)

Griffiths Drive in 1959, one of the main roads through the Ashmore Park Estate. This was the last of the 1950s estates to be completed. Ashmore Park was also named after a moated farmhouse which stood near to the present shopping centre where remains of the moat can still be seen. As on the Long Knowle and Moathouse estates several roads were named after councillors. Harry Griffiths, a local builder, was Chairman of the UDC in 1942 and Alan Griffiths, also a builder, in 1961. (C2/GRI/0/1)

Ashmore Farm photographed at the beginning of the twentieth century showing part of the moat still filled with water. Census information from 1891 shows the Lloyd family, headed by Sarah, a widow aged fifty four, living there with three of her children. However, the identity of the people in the photograph is not known. The original homestead stood inside the moat but this later farmhouse was situated to one side, close to the site of the modern Ashmore Inn. It survived for some time after the estate was built before being demolished. (Jim Evans, L8/ASH/E/1)

209

The Wyrley & Essington canal looking east from Pinfold's Bridge around 1930. The house on the left is 'The Hills' built in 1914 for Alfred Squire. The canal was built in 1797 to link Wolverhampton with the mines on the developing Cannock Chase Coalfield 'to render the conveyance of coals, ironstone, limestone, corn and other products less expensive than at present'. Surveyed by William Pitt, it was nicknamed the 'Curley Wyrley' due to the roundabout route it follows around Wednesfield necessitating the construction of many narrow hump backed bridges in the area which were a hazard to traffic before they were rebuilt. (D7/WYR/32)

The Wyrley & Essington Canal looking west from Pinfold's Bridge around 1930. It is believed that this photograph and the one opposite were posed, possibly for a coal merchant's advertisement. The boats are not moving and do not have engines but there is no tug visible. It is unlikely that a horse would have pulled three boats and there is no mast where the tow rope would have been attached. (D7/WYR/33)

A reaping machine at work on Ashmore Farm in the early years of the twentieth century. Clearly everyone turned out to help with the harvest in the days when farming was more labour intensive than today. This part of Wednesfield remained largely rural until the housing estates were built in the 1950s although there was a colliery to the north of the farm. (Jim Evans, L8/ASH/E/2)

The Cash Bakery in the High Street around 1937. The staff pictured are, left to right: Miss Florence Doody, Miss Nesta Bucknall(?), Arthur Pocock, Miss Jouvain(?) Morgan. Arthur Pocock started the first cash bakery in Wolverhampton in the 1920s. By 1939 he had seven shops in Wolverhampton, Wednesfield and Heath Town. The Wednesfield shop closed down at the start of World War Two. (Jeffrey Pocock, L3/CAS/E/2)

Wednesfield Chainmakers pictured in the Orchard buildings which stood next to the canal in Graiseley Lane. The photograph dates from around 1930 and the people include; back row, left to right: Bill McConkey, Mr Lathe, John McConkey, Sidney McConkey. Middle row: Mavis Allcock, Mary Wapples, Mrs Vincent, Gladys Gray, Iris Turner. Front row: Peggy Bough, Miss Winifred Leeding, Gloria Pallant, Miss Brown, Miss Brown. (Mrs McConkey, L6/CHA/1)

Bowmans Harbour in the early 1990s with the Heath Town flats and Holy Trinity church in the background. Very little evidence remains of the coalmining which took place in Wednesfield in the nineteenth and early twentieth centuries. This site where Wednesfield meets Heath Town, opposite New Cross, was mined in the earlier period and has recently been mined again using the open-cast method. There has been a great deal of controversy about this, local people fearing that the site would be a pollution hazard. The land is being reclaimed at the moment. (B3/BOW/5)

Brockhouse Castings in 1959. The firm came to Wednesfield in 1936 and made naval fittings during the war. The factory was in Hall Street and employed 350 people in 1961. They were 'Manufacturers of Steel Castings of all descriptions up to 7 tons' according to an advertisement of 1965. A newspaper article in 1979 reported that the firm was modernising and specialised in making anvils among other products for the oil, aerospace and motor trades. The factory appears to have closed in the mid 1980s. (L6/BRO/E/2)

Prestwood Road Nursery in 1942. The boy on the extreme left of the back table (in front of the rocking horse) is Colin Danher aged four. Many nurseries were established during the Second World War to enable women to work in place of men who were away fighting. (Mrs Lee, I3/PRE/1)

Wednesfield Kindergarten School in 1930. The school was at 54 Graiseley Lane and the Principal was Miss G. Margaret Stokes assisted by Mrs Hunter and Miss Painting. Back row, left to right: Jim Morrish, Joan Day (nee Powell), Joyce Brocks, Fred ?, Muriel Pattinson, Royston Mountney, Jack Gard. Middle row: G. Day, -?- , Margaret Saunders, Derek Critchley, Marguerite Elwell, -?- , Bessie Ketland. Front Row: Gordon Stagg, -?-, ? Lingard, Derek Lingard, -?- , Evelyn Marston. (Miss K.M. Saunders, Y5/WEDK/1)

Corpus Christi Primary School, Ashmore Park The entire school lines up for a photograph to go into the booklet issued for the official opening in May 1963. All of the photographs for the booklet were taken by John Beswick.

111

Junior Class 2 photographed in their classroom at the newly opened Corpus Christi Primary School, from the booklet for the official opening. (John Beswick)

The front entrance of Corpus Christi Primary School from the same booklet. (John Beswick)

Pupils at St Thomas' School in 1926/27. Back row: Hill, Molineux, Leeding, Wall, Adey, Swatman, Allcock, Smith, Adey. Third row: Crane, Gilbert, Green, Day (G.), Dillon, Day (N.), Dudley. Second row: Ashton, Simmons, Hillet, Allen, Whitehouse, Colebatch, Upton, Toombs, Beard. Front row: Tench, Bowyer, Payton, Kay, Nicholls, Jones, Leeding, Neal. A school was established in New Street in 1837 funded partly by subscriptions collected by the incumbent of St Thomas'. This school was succeeded by a National (church) School which stood in Graiseley Lane, where the present flats stand, and opened in 1856. St Thomas' merged with a larger and newer school across the road in 1931 moving into their premises. The present St Thomas's School is in Mattox Road and the buildings in Graiseley Lane are occupied by St Patrick's RC School. (Norman Day, Y5/WEDST/3)

St Thomas' Church, a rare photograph from before 1902 when a fire caused much damage necessitating extensive rebuilding. It would seem likely that the children are from the nearby St Thomas' school. The church was built on the village green and consecrated in 1750 as a Chapel of Ease in the Deanery of Wolverhampton. Before that people from Wednesfield were obliged to travel to Wolverhampton for church services. (Jim Evans, E1/STTH/E/14)

The scene of devastation after the fire which occurred on 18 January 1902. Only the shell and part of the tower survived. One reason that the fire did so much damage was that the Wolverhampton Fire Brigade had to stop several times on the way to rest the horses! The log book of St Thomas' School recorded that all the schoolchildren were taken to see the ruins. (E1/STTH/I/4)

St Thomas' Church photographed from Graiseley Lane and showing the canal bridge and rebuilt church tower. It was common, around the turn of the century, to encourage school children to pose for photographs. (DX/15, St Thomas' Church)

The interior of St Thomas' Church showing the rood beam that was erected in 1918 in memory of the 123 men from Wednesfield who died during the First World War. The original St Thomas' only had seating for fifty people. (E1/STTH/I/18)

WOLVERHAMPTON WORKHOUSE
(Built, 1900 - 1901).

Area of Union is 11,147 acres, including the Borough of Wolverhampton and the Parishes of Bilston, Short Heath, Willenhall, Wednesfield and Heath Town.

Rateable value of Union, £528,201.

Population of Union (1901), 154,581.

Numbers chargeable on June 14th, 1902:—Indoor Poor (excluding vagrants), 942; Cottage Homes, 208; Poor persons in receipt of Out-Relief, 3,229; Lunatics, 418; Total, 4,797.

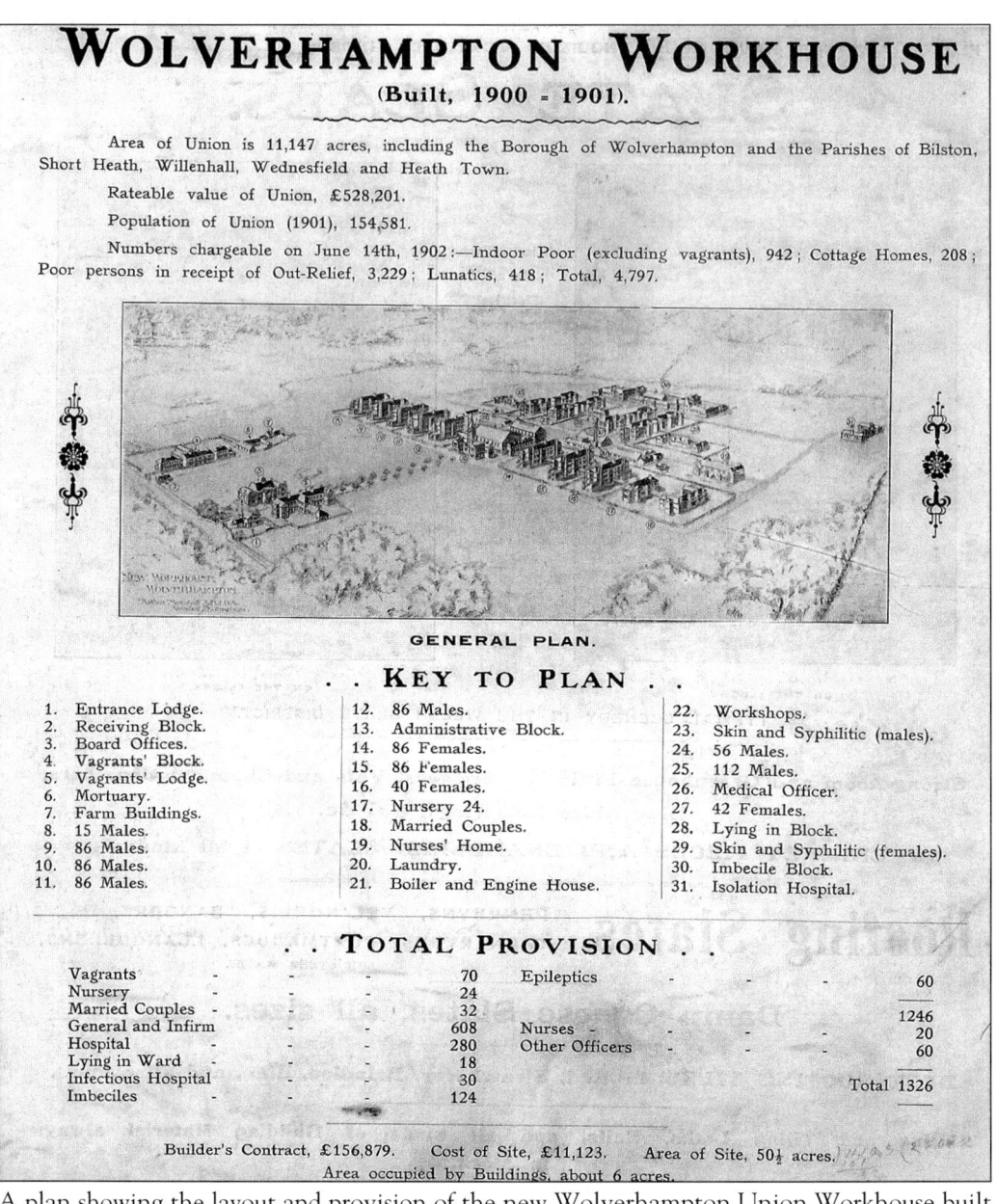

GENERAL PLAN.

. . KEY TO PLAN . .

1. Entrance Lodge.	12. 86 Males.	22. Workshops.
2. Receiving Block.	13. Administrative Block.	23. Skin and Syphilitic (males).
3. Board Offices.	14. 86 Females.	24. 56 Males.
4. Vagrants' Block.	15. 86 Females.	25. 112 Males.
5. Vagrants' Lodge.	16. 40 Females.	26. Medical Officer.
6. Mortuary.	17. Nursery 24.	27. 42 Females.
7. Farm Buildings.	18. Married Couples.	28. Lying in Block.
8. 15 Males.	19. Nurses' Home.	29. Skin and Syphilitic (females).
9. 86 Males.	20. Laundry.	30. Imbecile Block.
10. 86 Males.	21. Boiler and Engine House.	31. Isolation Hospital.
11. 86 Males.		

. . TOTAL PROVISION . .

Vagrants - - -	70	Epileptics - - -	60
Nursery - - -	24		
Married Couples - - -	32		1246
General and Infirm - - -	608	Nurses - - - -	20
Hospital - - -	280	Other Officers - - - -	60
Lying in Ward - - -	18		
Infectious Hospital - - -	30		
Imbeciles - - -	124	Total	1326

Builder's Contract, £156,879.   Cost of Site, £11,123.   Area of Site, 50½ acres.
Area occupied by Buildings, about 6 acres.

A plan showing the layout and provision of the new Wolverhampton Union Workhouse built on the boundary between Wednesfield and Heath Town. The previous workhouse had been on the corner of Steelhouse Lane and Bilston Road. One reason for moving was to gain land for a farm that would be worked by the inmates and provide food for the institution. Local people can still remember seeing the occupants of the vagrants block waiting by the side of the road for the doors to be opened so that they could claim a bed for the night. Only a few of these buildings still survive as part of the present New Cross hospital. (J4/NEW/E/3)

The infirmary at New Cross Workhouse, Christmas 1912. New Cross changed from a workhouse with an infirmary to a hospital over time. By the 1930s an X-ray department and pathology laboratory had been built. In 1939 it was classified as an A1 Hospital under the Emergency Medical Services Scheme and treated patients from the Services. In July 1948 when the National Health Service was set up it became part of the Wolverhampton Hospital Group. (Alex Chatwin, J4/NEW/I/3)

The Cottage Homes, built in 1889 in Amos Lane. They were built to house children whose parents were not able to support them. In many cases one or both of the parents were in the workhouse and before the Cottage Homes were built the children would also have gone into the workhouse and been separated from their families. (J4/COT/E/7)

The Girl's Home Yard around 1900. The Homes covered twenty acres and the children were housed in seperate buildings known only by a number. Although clearly an attempt to offer a more homely environment than that of the workhouse they appear very austere by today's standards. (J4/COT/E/2)

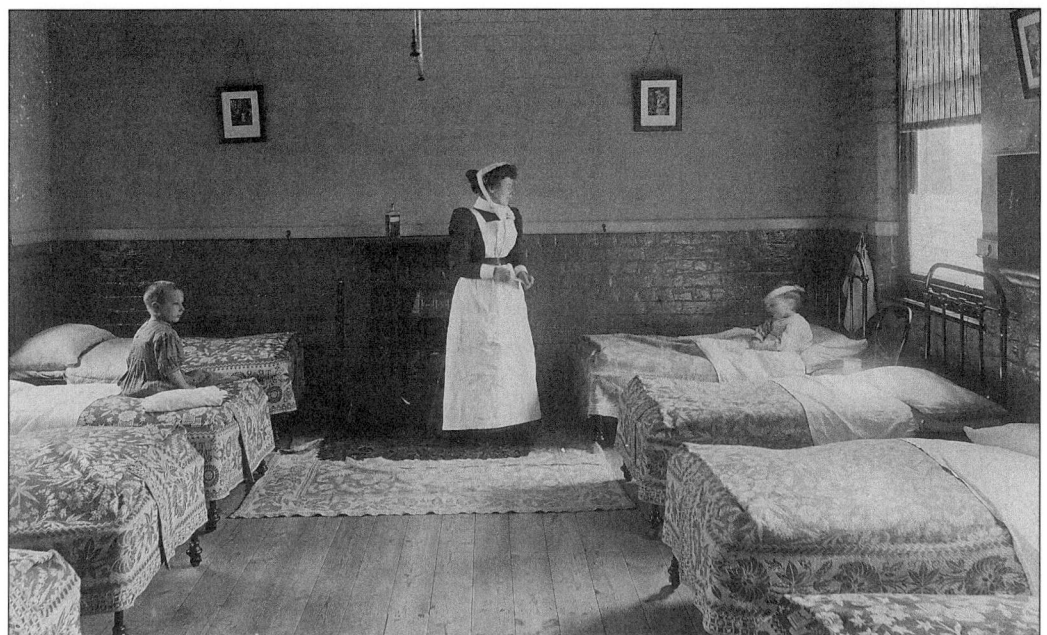

The Dormitory around 1900. The Homes complex included a school and an infirmary. Although this photograph is labelled 'Dormitory' the bandage on the boy's head would suggest it could have been the infirmary. The lady is wearing a uniform that could have been that of a nurse or workhouse matron. (J4/COT/I/4)

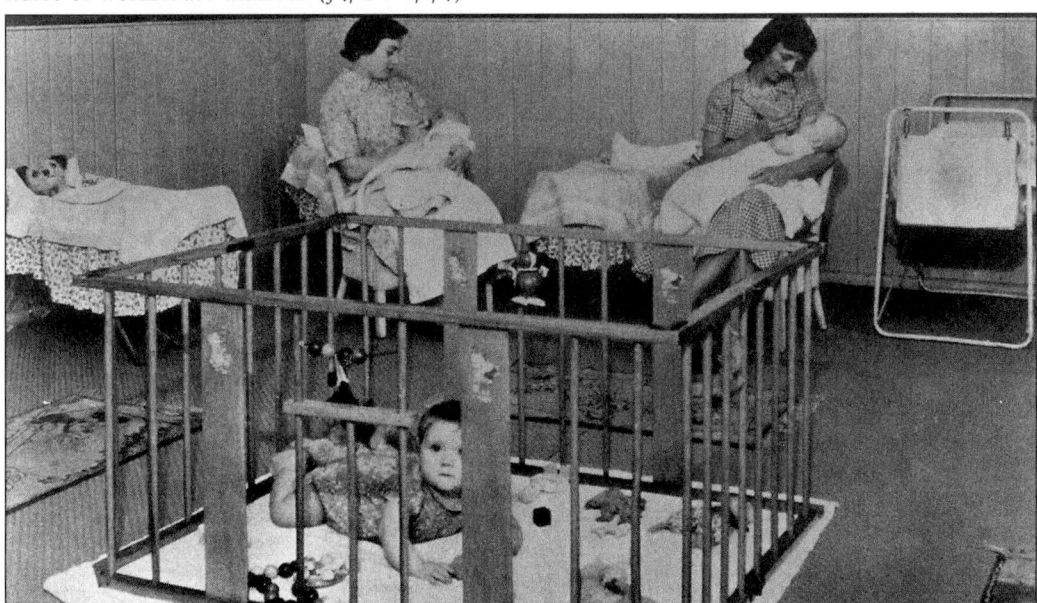

The nursery in one of the Cottage Homes taken from the Wolverhampton Official Handbook 1956. By this time the workhouse system had long gone but the council still provided places for up to one hundred children who needed temporary accommodation for whatever reason. By this time the children were attending local schools and no longer wore a uniform that made it obvious that they were from the Cottage Homes. By the end of the 1960s the buildings were being used for different purposes and they have all now been demolished. (J4/COT/I/10)

The Woodhayes Public House, Wood End Road, pictured in the Butler's Brewery magazine in September 1957. William Butler first started brewing in Wolverhampton in the 1840s. In 1873 he moved to new premises and established the Springfields Brewery part of which still stands although no longer in use. In 1957 Butlers owned over 800 freehold licensed premises in the area and had recently resumed an ambitious programme of rebuilding its pubs which had been interrupted by the war. The Woodhayes was apparently quite new when this photograph was taken. (L4/WOD/E/1, L4/WOD/I/1)

The Red Lion, Amos Lane, another Butler's Public House. Maps indicate that it was built at the junction with Prestwood Road between 1938 and 1955. In the early 1950s the landlord, Harry Davenport, hosted an annual Rose Show open to members of the Gents Smoke Room. (L4/RED/E/1)

The Dog and Partridge in 1977. This High Street public house, despite its mock tudor paintwork, is actually one of the oldest buildings in Wednesfield and has been licensed premises since at least 1782 when it was kept by Samuel Marston. It has recently been extended and refurbished and some of the ancient features have been highlighted. It retains a homely atmousphere with small rooms and ranges etc. (L4/DOGA/E/6)

Wednesfield Home Guard around 1941 outside the premises of Jenks & Cattell. Only one name is known; Charles William Haynes sits on the second row, sixth from the right. On 27th January 1941 No 1 'A' (Wednesfield) Company became the Willenhall and Wednesfield Battalion (later the 26th Battalion). The commanding officers were, successively, Mr C.E. Nelson, Mr H.S. James and Lt-Colonel A.T. Champion. (Colin Haynes, Y9/WED/1)

Wednesfield Football team around 1950. Back row, left to right: -?-, A. Clift (manager), S. Hayes, Pat Pioli, George Habberley (secretary), Arthur Stanley, Ken Jones, -?- , Sid Mattox, Bert Benton, Jack Smith, Bill Tandy, Ben Wear, ? Gethin, George Edmunds. Front: -?-, Alan Barnett (referee), George Stokes, Bill Joyce (chairman), Charles Wright, Stan Banks, R. Sambrook, ? Bickley, ? Bowen. Wednesfield FC was formed in 1946 and played in Division 1 of the Wolverhampton Amateur League. Home matches were played on the King George's Playing Field. (Stan Hayes, Y8/WEDF/2)

A float taking part in the Wednesfield Carnival on the Lichfield Road opposite to the present Wednesfield Village School. The board reads 'Tis a far far better thing that which I do now than I have ever done. A far better rest than I have ever known'. In the 1950s the carnival took place on the first Saturday in July and the floats were judged in several different categories with as many as forty entries. (Mrs Millington, V4/WED/7)

Wednesfield Operatic Society production of *Iolanthe* in the mid-1930s. (Freda Easthope, Y8/WEDO/3)

St Thomas' Mothers' Union on an outing to Dovedale in 1951. Left to right: Mrs Purshouse, Tom White, Revd Harry Baylis, Mrs Hamlin, Clarence Haden, Evelyn Stride, Mrs Manby, Fred Stride, Percy Alcock, Mr Manby, Cath Randle, -?- , Mrs Guy, Arthur Adey, Lavinia Turrell, Mrs Adey (in hat), Doris Barnes, Zak Purshouse, Gertie White, Mrs Humphries, Bert Barnes, Annie Day, Tommy Turrell, Mrs Proffitt, George Humphries (sanitary inspector), A. Proffitt. Front: George Yerrington, Jean Mallows, Roger Mallows (toddler), Howard Mallows, Muriel Munslow (nee Day), Mr Hamlin, Harold Randle. (Mrs Millington, Y2/STTH/1)

Wednesfield Trolley Bus Number 2 at New Cross in the 1920s travelling towards Wolverhampton. The trolley bus is passing tower wagon DA1350 used for making repairs to the overhead wires. A fleet of six trolley buses started running from Broad Street to Wednesfield in October 1923. They had to be single decker buses due to the low height of the railway bridge at the start of the Wednesfield Road. They terminated at Pinfold Bridge. The overhead wires were only twelve inches apart on this route until they were converted to the more normal eighteen inches in 1930.

Two photographs of the High Street taken in 1959 and showing how congested the street was before the old buildings were replaced. The top photograph shows St Thomas' church on the left and the one below it shows the church in the background. Wednesfield post office is on the left of the lower photograph and a Butler's Brewery Wagon can be seen in the background. (C1/HIGH/8/8), (C1/HIGH/0/7)

A Lorain tram stops a few yards from the Wednesfield boundary. These trams that took electricity up from studs in the road ran on this route from 1904 and continued on an overhead system from July 1921 until July 1923. They were also single decked and had to terminate before the canal bridge in Rookery Street which was too narrow and not strong enough to bear their weight. This tram is showing the abbreviation Raily Station on its indicator. The photograph would appear to date from the early years of the twentieth century. (Stan Webb)